Momentum Machines

Momentum Machines

Matthew Petchinsky

1

Momentum Machines: Small Habits Designed to Snowball into Unstoppable Forward Motion

By: Matthew Petchinsky

Disclaimer

This book, *Momentum Machines – Small Habits Designed to Snowball into Unstoppable Forward Motion*, is intended solely for **educational and inspirational purposes**. It is designed to help readers explore ideas, strategies, and reflections related to psychological growth, motivation, and lifestyle improvement. The content herein is based on research, personal development frameworks, and creative synthesis meant to encourage positive behavioral change and personal renewal.

However, **this book is not medical, psychological, or therapeutic advice**, nor is it a substitute for professional diagnosis, treatment, or counseling. The author is not acting as a licensed healthcare provider, psychologist, financial advisor, or therapist. Every individual's circumstances, health conditions, and psychological needs differ; therefore, readers should **consult qualified professionals** before implementing any recommendations or making changes to health routines, mental wellness practices, or financial strategies.

While every effort has been made to ensure the accuracy and usefulness of the information provided, results are not guaranteed, and the author assumes no liability for any outcomes that may arise from the application or interpretation of this material. By reading this book, you acknowledge full personal responsibility for your own decisions, actions, and results.

This work is meant to empower, not prescribe. It invites readers to **adapt ideas thoughtfully**, **exercise discernment**, and **use these principles as tools** to build sustainable momentum—one intentional step at a time.

Introduction

Great lives aren't built in leaps—they're **assembled in increments**. The legends, innovators, and changemakers of history didn't arrive at greatness through one monumental act. They arrived there through countless small, consistent movements—each one stacking atop the last until momentum became their ally instead of their obstacle. This book is designed to teach you that same science: how to **engineer momentum** so growth becomes automatic, and progress becomes inevitable.

Most people misunderstand transformation. They chase the breakthrough before building the base. They wait for inspiration before taking action. But **momentum doesn't come from motivation—it creates it.** Like a flywheel, the hardest part is the first push; once in motion, the system sustains itself. *Momentum Machines* helps you master that first push and transform it into continuous propulsion across every dimension of your life.

The concept of the "momentum machine" rests on one core truth: **every action compounds.** Habits are not isolated behaviors; they are interconnected gears in a personal growth engine. When you align your smallest daily behaviors with your deepest goals, friction drops, confidence compounds, and forward motion accelerates. Each act of focus, each minor improvement, becomes a micro-investment that pays exponential returns over time.

This book will walk you through a **psychological and mechanical framework for compounding growth**. You'll learn how to:

- Identify the micro-habits that yield the highest leverage in your personal and professional life.
- Replace willpower with systems that sustain themselves.
- Convert setbacks into momentum fuel by reframing failure as mechanical calibration.
- Create feedback loops that reinforce motivation and prevent stagnation.
- Build consistency not by effort, but by design.

Every principle in this book is crafted to show how small, intelligently chosen actions can become **self-reinforcing feedback loops**—just as gears in a machine transfer energy to each other. Over time, this creates what psychologists call **automaticity**: a state where effort feels effortless because your environment, habits, and self-image are aligned.

Momentum Machines isn't about hustle; it's about *architecture*. It's not about chasing productivity—it's about building a **perpetual growth engine** that carries you forward even when energy, time, or motivation run low.

By the end of this journey, you'll have the tools to construct your own momentum system—one that compounds discipline, multiplies opportunity, and eliminates inertia. Whether your goal is personal renewal, business growth, health mastery, or emotional resilience, this book is your blueprint for turning small, deliberate actions into unstoppable forward motion.

Welcome to *Momentum Machines*. It's time to **build your life like an engine—one calibrated habit at a time.**

Chapter 1: Micro Gears – Choosing Habits That Drive Other Habits

When you picture a machine, you don't imagine a single part moving in isolation. You imagine an intricate system of gears—each one interlocking, each motion transferring energy to the next. Your life works the same way. Every habit, no matter how small, either fuels or hinders another. The goal of momentum engineering is not to build *many* habits, but to build the *right* ones—those that act as **micro gears**, spinning others automatically into motion.

The Hidden Power of Micro Gears

Micro gears are not major habits like "run five miles every morning" or "write a book this month." They are *small initiators*—simple actions that reduce resistance and trigger other, larger habits without willpower. For example:

- Drinking a glass of water immediately upon waking is a micro gear that triggers hydration, metabolism, and mindfulness.
- Putting your workout clothes next to your bed the night before is a micro gear that removes friction from your morning fitness routine.
- Opening your task list while drinking your morning coffee is a micro gear that primes your brain for focus and execution.

These are not random actions; they are **strategic levers**. When chosen correctly, they start a domino effect where one small behavior automatically leads to another, creating a **self-reinforcing behavioral ecosystem**.

Habit Chains and Behavioral Compounding

Momentum doesn't depend on intensity—it depends on **continuity**. Every consistent habit forms a link in a chain that strengthens your behavioral identity. The more connected your habits become, the less effort it takes to sustain them.

In psychology, this is known as *habit stacking*: linking a new behavior to an existing one so it inherits its stability. But *Momentum Machines* takes it further. You'll learn to identify **keystone gears**—the small habits that, once set in motion, align several others automatically.

For instance:

- A daily "one-minute reset" (closing your eyes, breathing deeply, and asking, "What's my next best move?") can lead to better decision-making, emotional control, and focus.
- Writing a single line of gratitude before checking your phone can pivot your day's emotional tone and influence how you treat others.
- Tidying your workspace for sixty seconds each evening can lead to higher morning productivity, less overwhelm, and greater creative flow.

Each of these habits has **downstream effects**—they act as multipliers, not isolated tasks. When practiced together, they form the **momentum network** that drives exponential growth.

The Psychology Behind the Gear Effect

Humans crave momentum because it provides both direction and reward. Dopamine, the neurotransmitter responsible for motivation, spikes not when we achieve a goal but when we *move toward* it. Micro gears leverage this neurochemical truth by giving you **quick wins** that reinforce consistency.

Each time you complete a micro habit, you build a "success micro-dose." Your brain begins to associate progress with pleasure, transforming discipline into desire. Over time, this rewires your default behavior patterns. What once required conscious effort becomes *subconscious propulsion*.

The more micro gears you set into motion, the more effortless growth becomes. It's the psychology of the flywheel: the beginning is hardest, but every rotation builds stored energy. Once that energy reaches critical mass, momentum takes over.

Designing Your Micro Gear System

Start by mapping out your **core goals**—the areas of your life where growth would have the most ripple effect (e.g., health, finances, relationships, creativity, mindset). Then, identify one small behavior that directly influences each.

Ask yourself:

- What's the smallest, most repeatable action I can take daily in this area?
- Which behavior naturally triggers others without requiring motivation?
- What can I do that's so easy I can't fail to start?

From these answers, select 3–5 *micro gears*. Anchor them to consistent cues—times, locations, or existing habits—and run them for 21 days. Observe what new behaviors start to follow without deliberate effort. That's the sign your gears are interlocking.

Examples of Micro Gears:

- One deep breath before responding in conversation → builds patience, empathy, emotional regulation.
- Writing down one unfinished task before bed → builds clarity, stress management, and next-day readiness.
- Standing up every hour → builds posture awareness, blood flow, and focus renewal.
- Complimenting one person daily → builds social confidence, positivity, and emotional intelligence.

Each micro gear, when reinforced, becomes a **momentum amplifier**.

Journal Prompts for Reflection

1. What three areas of my life feel most stagnant or inconsistent right now?
2. Which small, repeatable actions could reduce friction in these areas?
3. When during my day do I already have consistent routines I could attach new habits to?
4. What behavior do I perform daily that could become a launch point for a better habit?
5. How do I usually feel after completing a small but meaningful action?
6. Which habits currently drive others in my life—positively or negatively?
7. What is one micro gear I can implement immediately after waking up?
8. What habit do I want to stop relying on willpower to maintain?
9. What physical cues (locations, objects, times) could help remind me of my new micro gears?
10. How can I celebrate or acknowledge each successful micro action to reinforce momentum?

Closing Reflection

Momentum is not an event—it's an environment. By selecting micro gears that naturally propel each other, you create a living system that moves even when motivation falters. The true secret of unstoppable individuals isn't their discipline—it's their design.

When you learn to identify and install habits that drive other habits, you become the engineer of your own evolution. Every small motion becomes a mechanical act of progress. The day you stop chasing big leaps and start mastering the art of micro gears is the day you begin building unstoppable forward motion—one calibrated turn at a time.

Chapter 2: Friction Reduction – Designing Environments That Make Progress Inevitable

In every machine, friction is the invisible force that slows progress, wastes energy, and overheats potential. In human behavior, friction operates the same way—it's the subtle resistance between intention and execution. It shows up as clutter, distraction, emotional overload, or poor system design. The greater the friction, the slower the forward motion. The secret to sustainable growth isn't adding more effort—it's **removing resistance** so progress flows naturally.

Friction reduction is the **second law of momentum engineering**: make it easier to do what moves you forward, and harder to do what holds you back. The world's most successful individuals don't possess superhuman discipline; they design environments that make the *right behavior automatic.*

The Mechanics of Friction

Friction appears in two primary forms: **physical** and **psychological.**

- **Physical friction**: tangible obstacles that make execution harder. Examples include disorganized workspaces, cluttered digital files, or energy-draining commutes.
- **Psychological friction**: invisible resistance within your mind—decision fatigue, anxiety, overthinking, or emotional associations that block action.

Each source of friction compounds. A messy workspace creates visual noise, which creates mental noise, which triggers avoidance behavior. A poorly designed routine demands constant willpower. Over time, that drag steals momentum from every area of life.

Just as engineers polish gears to minimize resistance, you must **smooth your environment**—physical, digital, emotional, and social—until progress becomes the path of least resistance.

The Law of Least Resistance

The brain naturally seeks energy efficiency. When two choices appear—one easy, one difficult—it unconsciously selects the easier option. Therefore, to make progress inevitable, you must **redesign your environment so that success feels easier than failure.**

For example:

- Keep your running shoes by the door, not buried in a closet.
- Store healthy snacks on your counter and hide junk food out of reach.
- Keep your notebook open on your desk, not tucked away in a drawer.
- Pre-load your workspace each night so morning focus requires zero setup.

You're not fighting laziness—you're working *with biology*. The easier an action feels, the more often it will be performed. Over time, these micro-optimizations compound into unstoppable consistency.

Environmental Architecture: Designing for Flow

To engineer momentum, design your surroundings like an ecosystem where every element supports forward motion. Your environment is not just a backdrop; it's a silent partner in your growth.

1. **Visual Triggers** – What you see dictates what you do. Place cues for your desired habits in plain sight. A filled water bottle signals hydration. A visible gratitude journal invites reflection. An open to-do list cues productive flow.
2. **Auditory Control** – Soundscapes shape emotion. Use quiet music, nature sounds, or white noise to cue focus. Mute notifications that fragment attention. Design your sound environment like an emotional thermostat.
3. **Spatial Flow** – Design your physical space to guide behavior through spatial zones. A "creation zone" for deep work, a "recovery zone" for rest, a "movement zone" for physical activity. Boundaries anchor routines.
4. **Digital Minimalism** – Your devices can either amplify your focus or fracture it. Audit your digital world:
    - Remove unnecessary apps.
    - Organize folders by function (Create, Learn, Relax, Maintain).
    - Use automation tools to reduce repetitive decision-making.
5. **Emotional Cues** – Surround yourself with symbols of progress: inspiring quotes, vision boards, books that resonate with your goals. Every visual cue should speak momentum.

Friction Mapping: Finding and Fixing Energy Leaks

Before you can reduce friction, you must first identify where it hides. Friction mapping is a process of diagnosing where effort leaks out of your system.

Step 1: List your three most important daily goals.
Step 2: For each, note where you feel hesitation, procrastination, or fatigue.
Step 3: Identify the *barrier*—is it environmental (e.g., clutter), emotional (e.g., fear), or procedural (e.g., no clear first step)?
Step 4: Simplify, automate, or eliminate.

Example:

- You avoid writing because your workspace feels chaotic. → Simplify: declutter, pre-set your tools.
- You avoid working out because the gym feels far. → Automate: switch to home workouts or morning walks.
- You procrastinate on tasks that lack structure. → Eliminate friction by using pre-built templates or checklists.

Momentum grows when **you remove instead of add**. Each source of friction removed returns time, energy, and focus to your growth engine.

The Psychology of Effortless Action

The less energy it takes to start a behavior, the more likely it is to become habitual. This is known as the **activation energy principle**. In chemistry, activation energy is the minimum energy required to trigger a reaction. In psychology, it's the energy required to initiate action.

When you lower activation energy—by preparing your environment, simplifying choices, and removing barriers—you make **action automatic**. This is why friction reduction works: it transforms behavior from an act of will into a natural reflex.

Your goal is not to constantly motivate yourself, but to **engineer conditions where the right action happens by default.**

Practical Systems for Friction Reduction

1. **The Two-Minute Reset Rule:** Anytime a task feels overwhelming, commit to doing it for two minutes. Most resistance vanishes once motion begins.
2. **The Default Setup:** Keep your tools ready for your next session before ending the current one. A pre-set workspace kills hesitation.
3. **Decision Templates:** Create pre-made routines for common scenarios (e.g., "If tired, then walk and stretch for five minutes").
4. **Energy Zoning:** Match your hardest tasks with your highest energy hours; automate or batch low-energy tasks.
5. **Exit Barriers for Bad Habits:** Add small frictions to stop negative momentum (e.g., uninstall a distracting app, keep unhealthy snacks out of reach).

Every adjustment should either **reduce friction for the good** or **add friction to the unhelpful**. Together, these shifts form a **momentum-favorable environment**.

Journal Prompts for Reflection

1. What daily tasks or goals currently feel harder than they should?
2. Where in my physical space does clutter or disorganization slow me down?
3. Which environmental cues (sights, sounds, or smells) motivate me most?
4. What behaviors drain my energy due to unnecessary friction?
5. What small change could make my most important habit easier to start?
6. Which distractions consistently derail my focus, and how can I remove them?
7. How can I create a "friction-free zone" for my top priorities?
8. What small barrier could I introduce to reduce a bad habit's frequency?
9. What does my ideal low-friction day look like from morning to night?
10. How can I re-engineer my environment tonight so tomorrow's progress happens automatically?

Closing Reflection

Progress is not a matter of pushing harder—it's a matter of **smoothing the path**. When friction is reduced, effort transforms into ease, and consistency becomes natural. You begin to experience flow—not because life gets simpler, but because *you've designed it that way.*

The most successful people don't fight resistance; they **engineer inevitability**. Every simplified decision, every pre-set environment, every frictionless process becomes a quiet accelerator of progress.

When your environment begins to work *for* you instead of *against* you, your habits evolve from mechanical effort into graceful motion. This is the art of friction reduction—transforming the machinery of your life into a system so efficient that progress stops being a struggle and becomes your default state.

Chapter 3: Feedback Fuel – Using Small Wins as Energy for Larger Goals

Progress is not powered by giant leaps—it's sustained by continual confirmation that motion matters. Every small victory is more than an achievement; it's **fuel**. In the mechanics of momentum, *feedback* is what keeps the machine alive. Without it, effort becomes guesswork, motivation fades, and movement stalls. But when feedback loops are harnessed consciously, they transform ordinary effort into **self-reinforcing propulsion**—a psychological energy source that multiplies itself through visible proof of progress.

The human mind is designed to seek evidence that it's on the right path. Each micro-success releases dopamine, the brain's chemical signal for reward and momentum. That feeling of satisfaction after completing even a small task isn't trivial—it's biological feedback saying, *"Continue. You're moving in the right direction."* The art of using feedback as fuel means capturing that signal and converting it into **forward momentum that scales upward**—from micro habit to master goal.

The Science of Feedback: Why Small Wins Matter

Our brains are terrible at perceiving incremental progress. Because transformation happens gradually, most people abandon their goals when they can't *see* progress quickly enough. The key to long-term success is learning to design systems that **make invisible progress visible.**

In neuroscience, this is tied to **reward prediction error**—the brain's measurement of whether an outcome was better or worse than expected. When you experience a "win," no matter how small, your brain records it as a success pattern and strengthens the neural pathways that produced it. Over time, repetition of small successes creates a psychological state known as *positive expectancy*—the expectation that effort leads to reward.

That expectancy becomes **momentum fuel**. It drives persistence, reduces fear of failure, and builds a deep emotional connection to your process.

In short:

- Small wins trigger dopamine.
- Dopamine builds motivation.
- Motivation reinforces action.
- Action produces more wins.
- Wins generate more dopamine.

That cycle is the **feedback engine**—a perpetual motion machine for growth.

From Reward to Reinforcement: The Feedback Loop Framework

To engineer momentum using feedback, you must convert your wins into reinforcement signals. A win uncelebrated is a gear left idle.

The framework has three layers:

1. **Detection** – Identify when a small success has occurred. This might be completing a chapter, choosing a healthy meal, finishing a work sprint, or following through on a promise to yourself.
2. **Acknowledgment** – Record or reflect on it. This solidifies it as *real evidence* that you're progressing.
3. **Amplification** – Leverage that emotional high to reinforce your identity: "I am someone who finishes what I start."

The loop strengthens the connection between identity and action. You no longer need to chase motivation—it becomes your default emotional state because success keeps confirming itself.

Micro-Wins That Matter

A micro-win is not just a task completed—it's a **signal that the system is working.** The key is to choose wins that reflect both effort and intention.

Examples of micro-wins:

- Writing one paragraph, not just thinking about writing.
- Drinking a full glass of water when you said you would.
- Starting your morning routine without checking your phone first.
- Completing a single workout rep when you didn't feel like exercising.
- Saying no to something that drains your energy.

Each micro-win builds *credibility with yourself.* Every time you follow through, your subconscious receives proof that you can be trusted to act in alignment with your goals. This self-trust compounds faster than any external validation.

Turning Feedback into Motivation Systems

You can systematize feedback so it becomes part of your momentum architecture. These are **practical mechanisms** for transforming data, reflection, and emotion into sustained propulsion:

1. **Visual Dashboards** – Use a habit tracker, progress chart, or journal log to make micro-wins visible. Seeing boxes checked creates psychological reinforcement.
2. **The Three-Minute Celebration Rule** – After every meaningful completion, take three minutes to celebrate intentionally. Smile, breathe deeply, stretch, or verbalize gratitude. Small celebrations anchor success in emotion.
3. **The Reflection Snapshot** – End each day by noting what worked and what didn't. Patterns of small victories reveal where momentum gathers naturally.
4. **The Feedback Flywheel** – Convert results into adjustments. If a habit sticks easily, double its frequency; if it resists, simplify it. Feedback isn't just confirmation—it's calibration.

Fueling Identity Through Micro Success

Every small win strengthens the narrative you tell yourself. When you repeatedly prove to yourself that you act on your goals, your *self-image* evolves from "someone who tries" to "someone who executes."

In behavioral psychology, this is the **identity feedback principle**: actions not only express who you are—they shape who you believe yourself to be. Once your identity aligns with your habits, discipline becomes effortless. You no longer push against resistance; your choices express your nature.

You can start reinforcing this alignment with small, verbal affirmations that connect each success to self-identity, such as:

- "I'm the kind of person who keeps promises to myself."
- "Momentum is my natural state."
- "Every small action today strengthens my future foundation."

The feedback you give yourself matters as much as the progress you make. Negative internal dialogue disrupts the loop; positive recognition sustains it.

Converting Setbacks into Feedback Fuel

Momentum engineering doesn't avoid failure—it repurposes it. Every obstacle, mistake, or delay contains informational feedback that can refine your system. When you view setbacks as *mechanical data* rather than personal defeat, they become **calibration moments**, not collapses.

Ask:

- What friction caused this resistance?
- Which micro-gear failed to engage?
- What system can I adjust so this doesn't recur?

By reframing setbacks as feedback, you remove shame and focus on system optimization. Even "failure" becomes a form of motion—redirected energy feeding back into improvement.

The Feedback Multiplier: Scaling from Micro to Macro

Once your micro-feedback loops stabilize, you can stack them into macro systems. For instance:

- Weekly summaries of achievements feed into monthly progress reviews.
- Monthly reviews guide quarterly goal recalibration.
- Quarterly outcomes determine long-term strategy shifts.

This creates **nested loops**—a fractal of progress where every layer reinforces the next. Small wins fuel medium goals, which power larger visions. This is how momentum transcends habit and becomes lifestyle infrastructure.

Journal Prompts for Reflection

1. What small wins did I achieve today that I've been overlooking?
2. How do I usually respond when I experience progress—do I acknowledge it or dismiss it?
3. What emotions do I associate with completing tasks or habits successfully?
4. How can I visually track or celebrate my small victories?
5. What area of my life would benefit most from daily feedback tracking?
6. When I fail or fall short, what story do I tell myself—and how can I reframe it as data?
7. Which small win from this week made me feel most confident? Why?
8. How can I make my environment reflect evidence of progress?
9. What would it look like if I treated feedback as fuel instead of judgment?
10. How can I design my own daily feedback ritual that guarantees momentum tomorrow?

Closing Reflection

Feedback is the heartbeat of progress. Without it, your efforts echo into silence; with it, every motion becomes a pulse of forward energy. The greatest achievers don't rely on endless motivation—they rely on **evidence loops** that remind them they're evolving.

When you learn to transform feedback into fuel, your smallest victories stop feeling small. They become sparks that ignite greater drive, courage, and consistency. Every micro-win whispers, *"Keep going—you're becoming unstoppable."*

By turning awareness into acknowledgment, and acknowledgment into reinforcement, you transform your growth system into a **self-charging engine**. Each success, however small, becomes part of an expanding network of proof that you can move mountains—one deliberate turn of the gear at a time.

Chapter 4: Compounding Motion – Letting Time Magnify Consistency

Momentum is not a burst of speed—it is the mastery of sustained motion. When you understand how time magnifies consistency, you stop chasing quick results and begin constructing systems that **compound progress.** Just as interest accumulates on invested capital, small, steady habits accumulate into extraordinary outcomes when given time to multiply. This is the principle of *Compounding Motion*—the quiet mathematics of success.

The laws of motion, psychology, and human behavior all share a universal truth: once an object—or a person—gains consistent velocity, less energy is required to keep it moving. The trick is not to sprint but to build a flywheel so steady that *momentum does the work for you.*

The Physics of Progress

Imagine pushing a massive flywheel: the first turn feels impossible. The second, slightly easier. By the tenth, the wheel starts turning on its own weight, storing energy from every previous effort. Eventually, you barely need to push—the system sustains its own motion.

That is how compounding works in your habits, health, creativity, or career. Each repetition doesn't merely add to your progress; it **multiplies** it. Each small win strengthens the system that makes the next win easier. You are not just moving forward—you are *building velocity.*

Consistency, then, becomes the **great amplifier of time.** The longer you maintain positive behavior loops, the more exponential your results become. Time is not your enemy; it is your ally—if you learn to use it.

The Mathematics of Momentum

At first, progress feels invisible. You show up, do the work, and see little return. But compounding doesn't reveal itself early—it hides behind patience. Like compound interest, the returns are microscopic at first and then explosive.

Here's the equation that governs *Compounding Motion:*

Consistency × Time = Momentum Growth²

Every consistent day adds mass to your momentum. Each repetition refines your systems, reinforces your identity, and reduces friction for the next round. Eventually, the graph curves upward, and growth becomes geometric rather than linear.

The mistake most people make is quitting during the *flat phase*—the quiet stretch when progress feels stagnant. But that phase is where foundation accumulates. Once time tips the balance, effort and outcome decouple; the same input begins producing **greater output.**

The Emotional Physics of Patience

Patience is not passive—it is *strategic stillness.* It's the discipline to trust your compounding system even when results are invisible. Impatience breaks the flywheel; patience feeds it.

To stay consistent long enough for time to amplify your effort, you must **shift your focus from outcome to rhythm.** Measure success by how faithfully you execute your system, not by what you immediately gain.

Ask yourself daily:

- Did I act in alignment with my system today?
- Did I maintain the motion, even slightly?
- Did I reduce friction instead of adding more?

If yes, you're compounding—even when you can't yet see the results.

Identity, Consistency, and Self-Trust

Every repetition is a statement about who you are. When you show up repeatedly, even imperfectly, you reinforce your *identity as a consistent person.* Over time, that self-trust becomes the most valuable fuel in your momentum engine.

Consistency also rewires your nervous system. Each repeated behavior strengthens the neural connections supporting it. Eventually, the behavior moves from effortful to automatic. This is *neural compounding*—the brain's way of turning repetition into instinct.

You no longer have to think about your habits; they think for you. That is when time begins to magnify everything you've built.

Designing for Longevity Instead of Intensity

Most people design habits for intensity—they start strong, push hard, and burn out. Compounding motion requires the opposite: designing habits for **longevity.** You're not building for next week; you're building for the next decade.

To do this, apply the **Three Principles of Sustainable Growth:**

1. **Simplify Early, Scale Later.** Start with small, maintainable actions. Complexity kills consistency. Once the pattern stabilizes, expand.
2. **Stabilize the System.** Ensure your environment, energy, and tools are optimized for continuity. A consistent 80% effort beats an unsustainable 110%.
3. **Automate Progress.** Create cues, checklists, and feedback systems that remove the need for daily decision-making. Automation is the infrastructure of momentum.

Each of these principles converts your finite energy into infinite endurance.

Time as a Growth Multiplier

Time doesn't change your results—it **amplifies** whatever pattern you practice. If you reinforce chaos, time compounds chaos. If you reinforce structure, time compounds stability.

Consider this:

- Reading 10 pages a day = ~12 books a year.
- Investing one extra hour a day in a skill = 365 hours of mastery annually.
- Saving $10 daily = $3,650 yearly, before interest.
- Writing 300 words daily = 100,000 words per year (the length of a novel).

Small consistent acts don't just *add up*—they *stack geometrically.* The longer you persist, the more massive your results become, and the less effort it takes to sustain them.

The most successful people aren't faster—they're simply **more consistent over more time.**

Resilience: Momentum's Hidden Partner

No machine runs forever without friction. Setbacks, fatigue, and interruptions will happen. The key is not to avoid them, but to recover quickly enough that momentum never fully stops.

Think of resilience as *momentum insurance.* It allows you to absorb shocks without dismantling the system. The faster you restart after a lapse, the less compounding you lose. Missing one day changes nothing; quitting for a month breaks the exponential curve.

Use the **24-Hour Recovery Rule:**

When you fall off your system—miss a habit, skip a day, lose focus—reset within 24 hours. This simple boundary keeps the compounding intact. Momentum thrives not in perfection, but in **prompt recovery.**

Visualizing the Compounding Curve

Imagine three individuals:

- **Ava** gives up after two months because results seem small.
- **Bryn** stays consistent for a year.
- **Caleb** continues for three years, adjusting and refining.

In year one, Bryn and Caleb's progress looks similar. In year two, Caleb's habits start multiplying effects—he's operating with momentum rather than effort. By year three, his results dwarf the others. The same effort, extended over time, creates **orders of magnitude more impact.**

That's the hidden geometry of compounding motion: **time doesn't just add—it multiplies the rate of addition.**

Practical Tools for Harnessing Compounding Motion

1. **The Momentum Ledger:** Track not your results, but your repetitions. Count consistency, not intensity.
2. **Micro-Adjustments:** Instead of overhauling your system, make 1% improvements weekly. These accumulate faster than radical changes.
3. **Momentum Reviews:** Once per month, analyze trends. Are you compounding or stagnating? Adjust friction points accordingly.
4. **The 90-Day Horizon:** View your habits in 90-day cycles. Each cycle represents a new layer of compounded strength.
5. **The Patience Mantra:** Repeat: *"My effort compounds, even when unseen."* This rewires your relationship with time.

These tools ensure that motion never dissipates—it accumulates like pressure in a sealed system, ready to expand exponentially.

Journal Prompts for Reflection

1. What habits in my life are already showing signs of compounding?
2. Where have I quit too early in the past because I couldn't see immediate results?
3. How does impatience show up in my routines, and what can I replace it with?
4. What's one area I could commit to consistent, small action for the next 90 days?
5. How do I measure success—by progress or by persistence?
6. What would my daily actions look like if I trusted time to amplify them?
7. What's one habit I can simplify to make it more sustainable long-term?
8. How can I build resilience into my system so setbacks don't derail me?
9. What's my "momentum recovery plan" for when I miss a day or fall behind?
10. How can I visualize or track my progress so I can *see* compounding in motion?

Closing Reflection

Compounding motion is the silent force that transforms ordinary consistency into extraordinary power. It is the alchemy of time, patience, and persistence—the invisible curve that turns small actions into monumental results.

When you surrender to time and align your daily rhythm with steady, deliberate effort, you no longer chase success—you *accrue* it. Your habits evolve into inheritance; your discipline becomes legacy.

Momentum is not about intensity, but endurance. The longer you keep your gears in motion, the less you have to push, and the more life begins to accelerate on your behalf. Let time be your silent collaborator, your greatest multiplier, and your most loyal ally.

Because once motion compounds, **you don't chase progress—progress chases you.**

Chapter 5: Maintenance Mode – Keeping Machines Running Through Change

Momentum is not a one-time achievement—it's a system that must be maintained. Every engine, no matter how powerful, requires tuning, lubrication, and rest to prevent burnout. The same is true for human beings. **Maintenance Mode** is the discipline of tending to your life's machinery so that consistency survives through disruption, stress, and evolution.

You cannot sustain forward motion if your systems—physical, mental, and emotional—begin to corrode. Maintenance is not weakness; it's strategic preservation. It ensures that progress continues even when the environment changes.

The Principle of Sustainable Motion

Every creator, leader, or high performer eventually encounters the paradox of progress: the faster you move, the more maintenance you require. Systems in motion wear down. Habits that once worked may no longer fit. The secret to unstoppable momentum is **learning to pause for recalibration without losing direction.**

Maintenance Mode is about staying operational during transformation. It's a deliberate rhythm of *inspection, repair, and optimization.*

When you master maintenance, change stops feeling like disruption and starts feeling like routine system upgrading.

Physical Maintenance – The Foundation of Function

Your body is the chassis that carries your momentum. It deserves the same care you would give any precision instrument. Neglect physical upkeep, and every other system—mental, emotional, or spiritual—loses efficiency.

Key Areas of Physical Maintenance:

1. **Sleep Regulation:** Sleep is not a reward; it's system calibration. Deep rest is where the brain clears waste, the body repairs tissue, and energy reserves reset. Maintain a consistent sleep schedule, even through transitions.
2. **Hydration and Nutrition:** Proper fuel allows the biochemical gears of focus and motivation to function smoothly. Hydration keeps electrical signals firing efficiently, while nutrient-rich food prevents system lag.
3. **Movement:** Muscles are motion generators. Stretching, walking, or strength training releases stored tension and boosts circulation—literal lubrication for the body's gears.
4. **Detox and Cleanout Practices:** Occasionally, your system benefits from internal maintenance. Some individuals find that **colon cleansing or medically approved enemas** (under professional guidance) can help alleviate digestive sluggishness and restore energy balance. Always consult a qualified healthcare provider before attempting such methods.
5. **Rest Cycles:** Schedule full-body resets—periods where you reduce workload, rest deeply, and allow biological systems to regenerate. True longevity arises from recovery discipline, not constant output.

Physical maintenance ensures your vessel doesn't overheat while chasing progress.

Mental Maintenance – Clearing the Cognitive Engine

Your mind is the processor that converts ideas into action. Over time, clutter builds up: unfinished thoughts, mental tabs left open, unresolved worries. Mental maintenance is the act of clearing that backlog so clarity and creativity can flow again.

Techniques for Mental Maintenance:

- **Digital Fasting:** Take regular breaks from screens and information intake. Information overload produces cognitive friction.
- **Single-Task Focus:** Choose one task and finish it. Multitasking scatters focus and drains your processing power.
- **Mindful Journaling:** Offload thoughts onto paper before they form mental congestion.

But the most powerful mental maintenance tool is meditation—**a recalibration of your mental machinery**.

Guided Meditation for Mental Maintenance

(10–15 minutes, once daily or as needed)

Step 1: Preparation

Find a quiet space. Sit comfortably with your spine straight but relaxed. Place your hands loosely on your knees or lap. Close your eyes and take a deep breath in through the nose for four counts, hold for two, and exhale through the mouth for six. Repeat this three times.

Step 2: Awareness of the System

Visualize your mind as a vast network of interlocking gears—each gear representing a thought, memory, or task. Some spin quickly, some slowly, some grind with resistance. You are the engineer observing them without judgment.

Step 3: Clearing Friction

Imagine warm golden light streaming down from above, flowing through your crown and cascading through each gear. As the light touches a gear, it begins to rotate smoothly. Notice the sound of the mechanism calming—the grinding replaced by a steady hum.

With each exhale, release a mental knot: a worry, a repetitive thought, or an outdated idea. See it dissolve in the light and vanish.

Step 4: Realignment

Now visualize the gears aligning perfectly in rhythm, one motion powering another. Whisper silently:

"My mind is a clear instrument. Each thought flows in harmony with my purpose."

Repeat three times.

Step 5: Return

Bring awareness back to your breathing. Inhale clarity, exhale tension. Wiggle your fingers, feel the present moment, and open your eyes.

After the meditation, write down one insight, emotion, or realization that surfaced. This integrates the clarity into conscious awareness.

Regular practice restores the **mental lubricant of focus**, allowing your ideas to glide smoothly into action.

Emotional Maintenance – Calibrating the Inner Circuitry

Your emotions are the current that powers your motivation. If left unmanaged, they can short-circuit your momentum. Emotional maintenance means honoring your feelings as data rather than distractions.

Core Components:

1. **Emotional Check-Ins:** Once daily, ask: *What am I feeling, and what does it need?*
2. **Expression Instead of Suppression:** Emotion is energy. Channel it—through writing, movement, conversation, or creative outlets—so it doesn't accumulate pressure.
3. **Boundary Calibration:** Protect your emotional energy from environments or people that drain your mental reserves. Maintenance includes knowing when to disconnect.
4. **Gratitude Rewiring:** Gratitude restores positive feedback loops, resetting your emotional operating system to abundance rather than scarcity.

Emotional maintenance is what keeps the engine resilient through uncertainty. It's not about suppressing your feelings—it's about *servicing them before they stall progress.*

The Rhythm of Regular Upkeep

Maintenance Mode is not a retreat from ambition—it's how ambition sustains itself. Just as machines undergo regular diagnostics, schedule your own personal inspections:

- **Daily:** Brief check-ins for physical state, mood, and focus.
- **Weekly:** Review your routines. What's running smoothly? What needs adjustment?
- **Monthly:** Identify system wear and tear—fatigue, resentment, imbalance—and apply resets.

Consistency in maintenance preserves both energy and enthusiasm. When you treat yourself as an intelligent system rather than an endless laborer, you build a life that runs *efficiently through every change.*

Journal Prompts for Reflection

1. What are the first signs that I'm due for maintenance (physical fatigue, mental fog, emotional irritability)?
2. How often do I schedule recovery, and how can I make it non-negotiable?
3. Which part of my system—body, mind, or heart—needs the most attention this week?
4. How do I currently manage mental clutter? What could improve this process?
5. What emotions do I tend to ignore, and how do they manifest later?
6. How does my physical health influence my creativity and decision-making?
7. What daily rituals could serve as my "reset buttons"?
8. When was the last time I felt fully recharged, and what conditions allowed that?
9. How can I incorporate mindful maintenance into my workdays without losing productivity?
10. What would my ideal *maintenance schedule* look like if I treated myself like a high-performance system?

Closing Reflection

Machines don't fail because they're weak—they fail because they go too long without care. The same is true for you. Maintenance is the art of honoring your limits so your potential remains limitless.

Physical upkeep keeps your vessel strong. Mental maintenance keeps your thoughts aligned. Emotional calibration keeps your motivation alive. When all three systems operate in harmony, your momentum becomes sustainable—even through chaos or change.

By choosing to maintain rather than ignore, you evolve from reactive to proactive—from burnout to balance. Momentum, after all, isn't just about moving forward; it's about **staying capable of motion**, no matter what life demands next.

Appendix A: Habit Loop Blueprint + 30-Day Momentum Tracker

Part I: The Habit Loop Blueprint

Every behavior operates through a simple neurological circuit known as the **Habit Loop**. Understanding and engineering this loop turns vague intentions into *mechanical reliability*. When mastered, it becomes the foundation of your personal momentum engine.

The loop has **three essential components**—*Cue, Routine,* and *Reward*—and a hidden fourth element: *Belief*.

1. Cue — The Trigger Mechanism

A cue is the environmental, emotional, or temporal signal that tells your brain to begin the habit.

- **Examples:**
  - Time-based: "It's 7:00 a.m., time to journal."
  - Location-based: "When I sit at my desk, I open my notebook."
  - Emotional-based: "When I feel anxious, I take three deep breaths."
  - Sequential-based: "After I brush my teeth, I prepare my water bottle."

Optimization Tip:

Make the cue **visible, consistent, and easy to act upon**. Cues are gears that initiate motion; design them intentionally instead of hoping they appear by chance.

Cue Engineering Checklist:

- Is it obvious?
- Does it occur naturally every day?
- Can it be linked to an existing behavior?
- Does it activate a positive state, not guilt?

2. Routine — The Behavioral Gear

The routine is the action itself—the repeatable process you want to install.

- **Examples:** drinking water, meditating, walking, writing, organizing, learning, or stretching.

The goal is not to make it perfect but **make it repeatable.** Start with a version so small that resistance can't exist.

Routine Engineering Formula:

If (cue) happens, then I will (routine) for (duration).

Example:

If I pour my morning coffee, then I will write one sentence in my journal for two minutes.

Over time, the brain begins to associate the cue with the routine automatically. This is **habit crystallization**—when an action stops being effort and becomes instinct.

3. Reward — The Reinforcement Circuit

Rewards are not indulgences; they're confirmation signals to your brain that effort was worthwhile.

Without them, the loop doesn't close—and the habit dies.

Rewards can be:

- **Intrinsic:** feeling calm, proud, focused, or accomplished.
- **Extrinsic:** checking a box, listening to a favorite song, or enjoying a ritual cup of tea.

The goal is to make the reward **immediate and emotionally satisfying**, because delayed rewards do not reinforce behavior.

Reward Design Prompts:

- What can I do immediately after the habit that feels good?
- How can I track visible progress (like a chart, streak, or progress bar)?
- How can I verbalize the success? (e.g., "That's one more brick laid in my future.")

4. Belief — The Self-Reinforcing System

Belief is the invisible force that keeps the loop alive during difficulty. It transforms behavior from an external task into an internal identity.

You're not "doing a habit"; you're *being someone consistent*.

Install Belief with Identity Statements:

- "I am a person who keeps promises to myself."
- "Momentum is my natural state."
- "I always move forward, even in small ways."

These affirmations stabilize your momentum loop against emotional turbulence.

5. Habit Loop Design Template

Component	Your Input	Optimization Notes
Cue	(Describe the trigger that starts your habit.)	Make it obvious and consistent.
Routine	(Describe the specific action you'll perform.)	Keep it short, concrete, and measurable.
Reward	(Describe how you'll celebrate or feel completion.)	Make it immediate and satisfying.
Belief Statement	(Affirm who you are becoming through this habit.)	Repeat it aloud after completion.

Complete this for each new habit before beginning your 30-Day Tracker.

Part II: 30-Day Momentum Tracker

The Momentum Tracker is your **visual feedback loop**—a log that turns invisible progress into visible evidence. You will use it to:

1. Observe patterns of consistency.
2. Identify friction points that interrupt your habits.
3. Strengthen belief through visible proof.

Each day equals one rotation of your momentum gear. Thirty rotations complete a full cycle.

Instructions

1. **Choose up to 3 micro-gears** (small habits) to track for 30 days.
2. Record completion daily using symbols:
   - ◈ = Completed
   - ◈ = Partial completion
   - ◈ = Missed
3. At the end of each week, write a *Reflection Note*—one sentence on what helped or hindered momentum.
4. After Day 30, analyze your streaks and identify your highest-leverage habits—the ones that make others easier.

30-Day Momentum Tracker Template

Day	Habit 1	Habit 2	Habit 3	Energy Level (1–10)	Reflection Note
1					
2					
3					
4					
5					
6					
7					
Week 1 Review: What worked best this week? What friction appeared?					
8					
9					
10					
11					

Day	Habit 1	Habit 2	Habit 3	Energy Level (1–10)	Reflection Note
12					
13					
14					
Week 2 Review: What micro-gear had the most ripple effect?					
15					
16					
17					
18					
19					
20					
21					

Day	Habit 1	Habit 2	Habit 3	Energy Level (1–10)	Reflection Note
Week 3 Review: What adjustments or simplifications improved consistency?					
22					
23					
24					
25					
26					
27					
28					
Week 4 Review: What success pattern do you see forming?					
29					

Day	Habit 1	Habit 2	Habit 3	Energy Level (1–10)	Reflection Note
30					

Post-Cycle Reflection Prompts

At the end of 30 days, complete these reflections to solidify your learning curve:

1. Which habit produced the greatest overall momentum?
2. What patterns emerged between energy levels and consistency?
3. Which cues were most reliable?
4. What friction points recurred, and how can they be reduced?
5. How has your belief in yourself evolved during this process?
6. What will you keep, change, or automate for the next 30-day cycle?
7. How did small wins affect your confidence in larger goals?
8. What systems or environments supported your success?
9. What emotional or physical benefits did you experience?
10. How will you celebrate the completion of this first momentum cycle?

Compounding the Next Cycle

Once you complete the first 30 days:

- **Retain your highest-impact habit** as a *core gear.*
- **Add one new habit** that connects naturally to it.
- Repeat the cycle with continuous reflection.

Over time, you will build a self-reinforcing architecture of small actions that interlock like gears—each month turning the next more smoothly, each habit strengthening the engine of progress.

Closing Note

Momentum is not built through pressure—it's engineered through pattern. The Habit Loop Blueprint and 30-Day Tracker are your schematics for that system.

Every checkmark, reflection, and micro-win becomes stored energy in your engine of growth.

Let this appendix be your maintenance manual: proof that small, deliberate motions—performed with awareness and tracked with care—can create unstoppable forward movement.

One rotation at a time, your machine becomes perpetual.

Message from the Author:

I hope you enjoyed this book, I love astrology and knew there was not a book such as this out on the shelf. I love metaphysical items as well. Please check out my other books:

-Life of Government Benefits

-My life of Hell

-My life with Hydrocephalus

-Red Sky

-World Domination:Woman's rule

-World Domination:Woman's Rule 2: The War

-Life and Banishment of Apophis: book 1

-The Kidney Friendly Diet

-The Ultimate Hemp Cookbook

-Creating a Dispensary(legally)

-Cleanliness throughout life: the importance of showering from childhood to adulthood.

-Strong Roots: The Risks of Overcoddling children

-Hemp Horoscopes: Cosmic Insights and Earthly Healing

- Celestial Hemp Navigating the Zodiac: Through the Green Cosmos

-Astrological Hemp: Aligning The Stars with Earth's Ancient Herb

-The Astrological Guide to Hemp: Stars, Signs, and Sacred Leaves

-Green Growth: Innovative Marketing Strategies for your Hemp Products and Dispensary

-Cosmic Cannabis

-Astrological Munchies

-Henry The Hemp

-Zodiacal Roots: The Astrological Soul Of Hemp

- **Green Constellations: Intersection of Hemp and Zodiac**

-Hemp in The Houses: An astrological Adventure Through The Cannabis Galaxy

-Galactic Ganja Guide

Heavenly Hemp

Zodiac Leaves

Doctor Who Astrology

Cannastrology

Stellar Satvias and Cosmic Indicas

Celestial Cannabis: A Zodiac Journey

AstroHerbology: The Sky and The Soil: Volume 1

AstroHerbology:Celestial Cannabis:Volume 2

Cosmic Cannabis Cultivation

The Starry Guide to Herbal Harmony: Volume 1

The Starry Guide to Herbal Harmony: Cannabis Universe: Volume 2

Yugioh Astrology: Astrological Guide to Deck, Duels and more

Nightmare Mansion: Echoes of The Abyss

Nightmare Mansion 2: Legacy of Shadows

Nightmare Mansion 3: Shadows of the Forgotten

Nightmare Mansion 4: Echoes of the Damned

The Life and Banishment of Apophis: Book 2

Nightmare Mansion: Halls of Despair

Healing with Herb: Cannabis and Hydrocephalus

Planetary Pot: Aligning with Astrological Herbs: Volume 1

Fast Track to Freedom: 30 Days to Financial Independence Using AI, Assets, and Agile Hustles

Cosmic Hemp Pathways

How to Become Financially Free in 30 Days: 10,000 Paths to Prosperity

Zodiacal Herbage: Astrological Insights: Volume 1

Nightmare Mansion: Whispers in the Walls

The Daleks Invade Atlantis

Henry the hemp and Hydrocephalus

10X The Kidney Friendly Diet

Cannabis Universe: Adult coloring book

Hemp Astrology: The Healing Power of the Stars

Zodiacal Herbage: Astrological Insights: Cannabis Universe: Volume 2

Planetary Pot: Aligning with Astrological Herbs: Cannabis Universes: Volume 2

Doctor Who: Convergence Protocol – The Replicator War

Nightmare Mansion: Curse of the Blood Moon

The Celestial Stoner: A Guide to the Zodiac

Cosmic Pleasures: Sex Toy Astrology for Every Sign

Hydrocephalus Astrology: Navigating the Stars and Healing Waters

Lapis and the Mischievous Chocolate Bar

Celestial Positions: Sexual Astrology for Every Sign

Apophis's Shadow Work Journal: **:** A Journey of Self-Discovery and Healing

Kinky Cosmos: Sexual Kink Astrology for Every Sign

Digital Cosmos: The Astrological Digimon Compendium

Stellar Seeds: The Cosmic Guide to Growing with Astrology

Apophis's Daily Gratitude Journal

Cat Astrology: Feline Mysteries of the Cosmos

The Cosmic Kama Sutra: An Astrological Guide to Sexual Positions

Unleash Your Potential: A Guided Journal Powered by AI Insights

Whispers of the Enchanted Grove

Cosmic Pleasures: An Astrological Guide to Sexual Kinks

369, 12 Manifestation Journal

Whisper of the nocturne journal(blank journal for writing or drawing)

The Boogey Book

Locked In Reflection: A Chastity Journey Through Locktober

Generating Wealth Quickly:How to Generate $100,000 in 24 Hours

Star Magic: Harness the Power of the Universe

The Flatulence Chronicles: A Fart Journal for Self-Discovery

The Doctor and The Death Moth

Seize the Day: A Personal Seizure Tracking Journal

The Ultimate Boogeyman Safari: A Journey into the Boogie World and Beyond

Whispers of Samhain: 1,000 Spells of Love, Luck, and Lunar Magic: Samhain Spell Book

Apophis's guides:Witch's Spellbook Crafting Guide for Halloween

Frost & Flame: The Enchanted Yule Grimoire of 1000 Winter Spells

The Ultimate Boogey Goo Guide & Spooky Activities for Halloween Fun

Harmony of the Scales: A Libra's Spellcraft for Balance and Beauty

The Enchanted Advent: 36 Days of Christmas Wonders

Nightmare Mansion: The Labyrinth of Screams

Harvest of Enchantment: 1,000 Spells of Gratitude, Love, and Fortune for Thanksgiving

The Boogey Chronicles: A Journal of Nightly Encounters and Shadowy Secrets

The 12 Days of Financial Freedom: A Step-by-Step Christmas Countdown to Transform Your Finances

Sigil of the Eternal Spiral Blank Journal

A Christmas Feast: Timeless Recipes for Every Meal

Holiday Stress-Free Solutions: A Survival Guide to Thriving During the Festive Season

Yu-Gi-Oh! Holiday Gifting Mastery: The Ultimate Guide for Fans and Newcomers Alike

Holiday Harmony: A Hydrocephalus Survival Guide for the Festive Season

Celestial Craft: The Witch's Almanac for 2025 – A Cosmic Guide to Manifestations, Moons, and Mystical Events

Doctor Who: The Toymaker's Winter Wonderland

Tulsa King Unveiled: A Thrilling Guide to Stallone's Mafia Masterpiece

Pendulum Craft: A Complete Guide to Crafting and Using Personalized Divination Tools

Nightmare Mansion: Santa's Eternal Eve

Starlight Noel: A Cosmic Journey through Christmas Mysteries

The Dark Architect: Unlocking the Blueprint of Existence

Surviving the Embrace: The Ultimate Guide to Encounters with The Hugging Molly

The Enchanted Codex: Secrets of the Craft for Witches, Wiccans, and Pagans

Harvest of Gratitude: A Complete Thanksgiving Guide

Yuletide Essentials: A Complete Guide to an Authentic and Magical Christmas

Celestial Smokes: A Cosmic Guide to Cigars and Astrology

Living in Balance: A Comprehensive Survival Guide to Thriving with Diabetes Insipidus

Cosmic Symbiosis: The Venom Zodiac Chronicles

The Cursed Paw of Ambition

Cosmic Symbiosis: The Astrological Venom Journal

Celestial Wonders Unfold: A Stargazer's Guide to the Cosmos (2024-2029)

The Ultimate Black Friday Prepper's Guide: Mastering Shopping Strategies and Savings

Cosmic Sales: The Astrological Guide to Black Friday Shopping

Legends of the Corn Mother and Other Harvest Myths

Whispers of the Harvest: The Corn Mother's Journal

The Evergreen Spellbook

The Doctor Meets the Boogeyman

The White Witch of Rose Hall's SpellBook

The Gingerbread Golem's Shadow: A Study in Sweet Darkness

The Gingerbread Golem Codex: An Academic Exploration of Sweet Myths

The Gingerbread Golem Grimoire: Sweet Magicks and Spells for the Festive Witch

The Curse of the Gingerbread Golem

10-minute Christmas Crafts for kids

Christmas Crisis Solutions: The Ultimate Last-Minute Survival Guide

Gingerbread Golem Recipes: Holiday Treats with a Magical Twist

The Infinite Key: Unlocking Mystical Secrets of the Ages

Enchanted Yule: A Wiccan and Pagan Guide to a Magical and Memorable Season

Dinosaurs of Power: Unlocking Ancient Magick

Astro-Dinos: The Cosmic Guide to Prehistoric Wisdom

Gallifrey's Yule Logs: A Festive Doctor Who Cookbook

The Dino Grimoire: Secrets of Prehistoric Magick

The Gift They Never Knew They Needed

The Gingerbread Golem's Culinary Alchemy: Enchanting Recipes for a Sweetly Dark Feast

A Time Lord Christmas: Holiday Adventures with the Doctor

Krampusproofing Your Home: Defensive Strategies for Yule

Silent Frights: A Collection of Christmas Creepypastas to Chill Your Bones

Santa Raptor's Jolly Carnage: A Dino-Claus Christmas Tale

Prehistoric Palettes: A Dino Wicca Coloring Journey

The Christmas Wishkeeper Chronicles

The Starlight Sleigh: A Holiday Journey

Elf Secrets: The True Magic of the North Pole

Candy Cane Conjurations

Cooking with Kids: Recipes Under 20 Minutes

Doctor Who: The TARDIS Confiscation

The Anxiety First Aid Kit: Quick Tools to Calm Your Mind

Frosty Whispers: A Winter's Tale

The Infinite Key: Unlocking the Secrets to Prosperity, Resilience, and Purpose

The Grasping Void: Why You'll Regret This Purchase

Astrology for Busy Bees: Star Signs Simplified

The Instant Focus Formula: Cut Through the Noise

The Secret Language of Colors: Unlocking the Emotional Codes

Sacred Fossil Chronicles: Blank Journal

The Christmas Cottage Miracle

Feeding Frenzy: Graboid-Inspired Recipes

Manifest in Minutes: The Quick Law of Attraction Guide

The Symbiote Chronicles: Doctor Who's Venomous Journey

Think Tiny, Grow Big: The Minimalist Mindset

The Energy Key: Unlocking Limitless Motivation

New Year, New Magic: Manifesting Your Best Year Yet

Unstoppable You: Mastering Confidence in Minutes

Infinite Energy: The Secret to Never Feeling Drained

Lightning Focus: Mastering the Art of Productivity in a Distracted World

Saturnalia Manifestation Magick: A Guide to Unlocking Abundance During the Solstice

Graboids and Garland: The Ultimate Tremors-Themed Christmas Guide

12 Nights of Holiday Magic

The Power of Pause: 60-Second Mindfulness Practices

The Quick Reset: How to Reclaim Your Life After Burnout

The Shadow Eater: A Tale of Despair and Survival

The Micro-Mastery Method: Transform Your Skills in Just Minutes a Day

Reclaiming Time: How to Live More by Doing Less

Chronovore: The Eternal Nexus

The Mind Reset: Unlocking Your Inner Peace in a Chaotic World

Confidence Code: Building Unshakable Self-Belief

Baby the Vampire Terrier
Baby the Vampire Terrier's Christmas Adventure
Celestial Streams: The Content Creator's Astrology Manual
The Wealth Whisperer: Unlocking Abundance with Everyday Actions
The Energy Equation: Maximize Your Output Without Burning Out
The Happiness Algorithm: Science-Backed Steps to Joyful Living
Stress-Free Success: Achieving Goals Without Anxiety
Mindful Wealth: The New Blueprint for Financial Freedom
The Festive Flavors of New Year: A Culinary Celebration
The Master's Gambit: Keys of Eternal Power
Shadowed Secrets: Groundhog Day Mysteries
Beneath the Burrow: Lessons from the Groundhog
Spring's Whispers: The Groundhog's Prediction
The Limitless Mindset: Unlock Your Untapped Potential
The Focus Funnel: How to Cut Through Chaos and Get Results
Bold Moves: Building Courage to Live on Your Terms
The Daily Shift: Simple Practices for Lasting Transformation
The Quarter-Life Reset: Thriving in Your 20s and 30s
The Art of Shadowplay: Building Your Own Personal Myth
The Eternal Loop: Finding Purpose in Repetition
Burrowing Wisdom: Life Lessons from the Groundhog
Shadow Work: A Groundhog Day Perspective
Love in Bloom: 5-Minute Romantic Gestures
The Shadowspell Codex: Secrets of Forbidden Magick
The Burnout Cure: Finding Balance in a Busy World
The Groundhog Prophecy: Unlocking Seasonal Secrets
Nog Tales: The Spirited History of Eggnog
Six More Weeks: Embracing Seasonal Transitions
The Lumivian Chronicles: Fragments of the Fifth Dimension
Money on Your Mind: A Beginner's Guide to Wealth
The Focus Fix: Breaking Through Distraction

January's Spirit Keepers: Mystical Protectors of the Cold
Creativity Unchained: Unlocking Your Wildest Ideas in 2025
Manifestation Mastery: 365 Days to Rewrite Your Reality
The Groundhog's Mirror: Reflecting on Change
The Weeping Angels' Christmas Curse
Burrowed in Time: A Groundhog Day Journey
Heartbeats: Poems to Share with Your Valentine
Dino Wicca: The Sacred Grimoire of Prehistoric Magick
Courage of the Pride: Finding Your Inner Roar
The Lion's Leap: Bold Moves for Big Results
Healthy Hustle: Achieving Without Overworking
Practical Manifesting: Turning Dreams into Reality in 2025
Jurassic Pharaohs: Unlocking the Magick of Ancient Egypt and Dino Wicca
The Happiness Equation: Small Changes for Big Joy
The Confidence Compass: Finding Your Inner Strength
Whispers in the Hollow: Tales of the Forgotten Beasts
Echoes from the Hollow: The Return of Forgotten Beasts
The Hollow Ascendant: The Rise of the Forgotten Beasts
The Relationship Reset: Building Better Connections
Mastering the Morning: How to Win the Day Before 8 AM
The Shadow's Dance: Groundhog Day Symbolism
Cupid's Kitchen: Quick Valentine's Day Recipes
Valentine's Day on a Budget: Love Without Breaking the Bank
Astrocraft: Aligning the Stars in the World of Minecraft
Forecasting Life: Groundhog Day Reflections

Bleeding Hearts: Twisted Tales of Valentine's Terror

Herbal Smoke Revolution: The Ultimate Guide to Nature's Cigarette Alternative

Winter's Wrath: The Complete Survival Blueprint for Extreme Freezes.

The Groundhog's Shadow: A Tale of Seasons
Burrowed Insights: Wisdom from the Groundhog

Sensual Strings: The Art of Erotic Bondage
Whispered Flames: Unlocking the Power of Fire Play
Forgotten Shadows: A Guide to Cryptids Lost to Time
Six Weeks of Secrets: Groundhog Day's Hidden Messages
Shadows and Cycles: Groundhog Day Reflections
The Art of Love Letters: Crafting the Perfect Message
Romantic Getaways at Home: Turning Your Space into Paradise
Purrfect Brews: A Cat Lover's Guide to Coffee and Companionship
The Groundhog's Wisdom: Timeless Lessons for Modern Life
The Shadow Oracle: Groundhog Day as a Predictor
Emerging from the Burrow: A Journey of Renewal
The Language of Love: Learning Your Partner's Love Style
Authorpreneur: The Ultimate Blueprint for Writing, Publishing, and Thriving as an Author
Weathering the Seasons: Groundhog Day Perspectives
Valentine's Day Magic: A Guide to Romantic Rituals
The Shadow Chronicles: Stories of Groundhog Day
Love and Laughter: Fun Games for Valentine's Day
AstroRealty: Unlocking the Stars for Property Success
The Groundhog's Path: A Guide to Seasonal Balance
Groundhog Day Diaries: Reflections in the Shadow
The Groundhog's Light: Illuminating the Path Ahead
Valentine's Traditions from Around the World
AI Wealth Revolution: Unlocking the Trillionaire Mindset
Love Rekindled: Reigniting Passion in Relationships
Single and Thriving: Self-Love on Valentine's Day
Emerald Legends: Mystical Tales of Ireland
Green Alchemy: Harnessing Nature's Magic
The Hearts of Horror: A Valentine's Day Nightmare
The Leprechaun's Guide to Wealth and Wisdom
Dancing with the Sidhe: Celebrating the Otherworld

Shamrocks and Shadows: Mysteries of the Green Isle

Emerald Energy: Harnessing Luck and Growth

The Gingerbread Golem's Valentine: A Sweetheart's Guide to Love and Enchantment

The Celtic Knot: Weaving Life and Destiny

Green Fire: Elemental Magic for St. Patrick's Day

Clover Chronicles: Finding Your Inner Luck

Ireland's Mystical Creatures: A Field Guide

Gingerbread Golem's Love Almanac

Prowl and Thrive: The Lion's Guide to Success

Love Alchemy: Transforming Your Life Through Heart Energy

WORLD DOMINATION: Woman's Rule 3:The New Life

The Midnight Rose: A Guide to Lunar Love Spells

The Forbidden Letters: Writing Your Own Love Prophecy

Luck and Lore: St. Patrick's Day for Modern Mystics

The Green Path: A Pagan Celebration of Renewal

The Dark Architect's Guide to Reprogramming Reality

Prankster's Paradise: A Guide to Harmless Hijinks

Manifest Your Reality: The Law of Attraction Simplified

The TARDIS Owner's Manual: Understanding the Doctor's Ship: *A complete guide to the TARDIS, its technology, secrets, and mysteries*

Starlit Romance: Astrology Secrets for Finding True Love

The Time Lord's Atlas: A Complete Guide to the Whoniverse: ***A breakdown of the locations, planets, and dimensions explored in Doctor Who***

Sweetheart Shadows: The Dark Side of Love and Attraction

February Fire: Reigniting Passion in Every Area of Life

The Self-Love Toolkit: 5 Ways to Embrace Who You Are

February Sparks: Ignite Your Dreams in 28 Days

March to Success: A 31-Day Action Blueprint

Ancient Paths: The 13 Sacred Principles of Dino Wicca

Echoes of Tomorrow: Navigating the AI Revolution
The Wellness Blueprint: Balancing Mind, Body, and Soul
Green Horizons: Sustainable Living for a Better Tomorrow
The AI Wealth Code: How to Make Millions with Automation
AI-Powered Creativity: Writing, Art, and Music for Profit
Extinction Rites: Rebirthing Your Soul Through Prehistoric Magick
Sacred Serpents tarot
Celestial Enchantment blank journal
Star Strains
Culinary Journeys: Exploring Global Flavors at Home
The Hollowvale Curse
The Hollowvale Harvest
The Egg of Transformation: Awakening Your Inner Power
Blooming Into Power: A Wiccan Guide to Spring Awakening
The Nightmare Nexus: The Third Doctor's Perilous Haunting
Digital Detox: Reclaiming Your Life in a Connected World
Ostara's Path: Walking the Spiral of Renewal
The Sacred Hare
Financial Freedom: Building Wealth in the Modern Age
Spring's Cauldron: Stirring the Waters of Change
The Hollowvale Pact
Quantum Consciousness: The Science of Reality Shifting
The Hollowvale Hunger
The Sacred Waters Within: A Witch's Guide to Hydrocephalus Magick
The Raven's Nest: Building a Life of Unshakable Stability
AI and the Human Mind: The Future of Intelligence
The Hollowvale Reckoning
Timeless Love: Building and Maintaining Lasting Relationships
The Raven's Roar: Unlocking Unstoppable Confidence
Raven Sight: Awakening Intuition and Inner Wisdom

The Butterfly Effect: Small Changes, Big Transformations

Taming the Boogeyman: How to Conquer Your Inner Fears

The Magick of Green: Awakening Earth's Energy in You

The Entrepreneurial Mindset: Secrets to Business Success

The Hollowvale End

The Shadow Luck Ritual: Reclaiming Power from Your Dark Side

Spring Magick for Beginners: A Simple Guide to Seasonal Energy Work

Doctor Who: The Hollowvale Conundrum

The March of Miracles: Unlocking Synchronicities in Spring

Unveiling the Cosmos: A Guide to Stargazing and Space Exploration

The Ultimate Guide to Surviving an Economic Collapse

The AI Gold Rush: How to Profit from the AI Revolution

Bastet's Shadow: The Hidden Power of Feline Magick

The Bastet Codex: Unlocking the Goddess's Magickal Secrets

Purring Spells: Harnessing Bastet's Healing Frequencies

Bastet's Nine Lives: Rebirth, Transformation, and Immortality Spells

Primal Currents: Hydrocephalus Magick in the Path of Dino Wicca

The Digital Gold Rush: Mastering E-Commerce and Online Sales

Future Shock: Adapting to the Next Decade of Change

The Quantum Mindset: Think Like a Billionaire

Sacred Motherhood: Awakening the Divine Feminine Within

The Mother's Spellbook: Enchantments for Love, Protection, and Prosperity

The Witch's Guide to Parenting: Raising Empowered and Intuitive Children

The Magick of Motherhood: Reclaiming Your Power Through Rituals

The Pagan Path to Self-Love: A Goddess's Guide to Worth and Confidence
Wild Woman Magick: Unleashing Your Primal Power
The Money Magnet Blueprint: Unlocking Unlimited Wealth
Biohacking 101: Unlock Your Body's Full Potential
The Wild Father: A Pagan Guide to Strength and Wisdom
The Sacred Masculine: Unlocking Your Inner Power
The Druid's Compass
The Warrior's Mindset
The Father's Fire
Odin's Path
Ancestral Bonds
The House That Whispers
The Magician's Code
The Wild Hunt
The Green Man's Path
The Altar of Success
The Shadow and the Sword
The High Priestess's Guide to Energy Healing
The Lunar Mother
The Sacred Self-Care Grimoire
The Womb Wisdom Codex
The Wheel of the Mother
The Witch's Guide to Manifestation
The Q2 Reset
The Ultimate Guide to AI-Powered Passive Income
Escape the 9-5
AI Feline Fortunes
The Tear-Stained Grimoire
Razorblade Runes
Cemetery Sirens
The Midnight Wristwatch
The Town That Forgets

AI Horror & Creepypasta
The Hollow Frequency
The Breach Echo
The Quiet Between Worlds
The Sigil of Tharan-Khul
Summon the Vault of Y'ha'ten
The Becoming Codex
The Profit of Az'ra-nar
The Drowned Logos
Echoes of the Eldritch Will
The Deep Ledger
Necronomicon of Networth
Covenant of the Wealthwyrm
The Whisperer's Manifesto
The Rites of Azh-K'luth
The Ark of the Crawling Coin
The Tithe of Shadows
Inkheart Abyss
The Timewinds of Y'ha-nthlei
The Spiral Labyrinth of Azag-Nirrh
The Gallifreyan Heresy of the Black Pharaoh
The Psalms of Nyog-Sotha
Black Rain Alchemy
The Infinite Maw
The Entropic Blueprint
The Oracle of Sh'guul
The Book of Breach
The Drowned Saint's Testament
Dreamcraft of the Sleeper God
The Silence Market
Cthonomics: The Dark Wealth Algorithm
Invocation of the Ten-Eyed King
Wealthbound to the Wyrm Below

Become the Unnameable
Codex of the Sovereign Flame
Rituals of Relentless Becoming
The Shadow Ascends
The Eyes Beneath You
The Will That Wakes Worlds
Silence Is a Weapon
The Mirror That Screams
The Whisper Between Moments
The Mind That Devours Fear
The Myth of the Finished Self
The Architect of Your Madness
The Voice You've Buried
The Discipline of Madness
Stormborn: Awakening Your Inner Tempest
The Mind That Ate Time
Unbind Your Becoming
The Pact You Owe Yourself
The Devourer's Diet
The Acid That Carves the Path
The Tower You Must Burn
The Breath Between Worlds
Speak Like the Deep
The Labyrinth Within
The Spine of the Sea God
Rejection Is a Portal
The Crown You Refused
The Scar Is the Spell
The Lightless Flame
The Habit of Becoming Horrific
ChickenJockey Chaos
The Gatekeeper Within
You Are Not Your Name

The Compass of the Mad
The Archive of Unsent Letters
What the Mirror Can't Show You
The Knife You Needed
Worship Nothing, Become Everything
The Other Voice
The Body the World Forgot
The Vein of the Void
The Black Bone Codex
The Puzzle of the Hidden Self (Millennium Puzzle)
The Eye That Sees the Lie *(Millennium Eye)*
The Ring of Return (Millennium Ring)
The Rod of Relentless Will ***(Millennium Rod)***
The Tally of the Soul (Millennium Tauk/Necklace)
The Key to the Locked Timeline (Millennium Key)
The Scale of Sacred Decisions (Millennium Scales)
Inferno Bites: The UnOfficial Minecraft Lava Cookbook
Rot in the Attic
Prana: The Hidden Force of Your Infinite Self
The Shadow Realm Within: Transforming Darkness Into Destiny
The Borderland Collapse
Claws of Protection: Bastet's Defensive Magick
Mr. Ring-a-Ding's Madness
Yugioh Astrology: Celestial Deckcraft and Duel Destiny (2026–2027 Edition)
The Seal You Signed: Unlocking the Power You Once Feared
The Puzzle of Infinite Minds: Unlocking the Mentalism Hidden Within
The Eye That Mirrors the All: Secrets of Inner Reflection
Doctor Who: The Toymaker's Broadcast
The Rod of Eternal Flow: Commanding the Currents of Vibration

Golden Eyes of Bastet: Enhancing Psychic Vision
The Key of Dual Forces: Balance Within the Polarity
The Scales of Living Rhythm: Timing the Dance of Life
The Necklace of Hidden Cause: Weaving the Webs of Fate
The Ring of Secret Masters: Rising Through the All Within All
Daggers of the Dying Deep
Bastet's Wealth and Fortune Magick: Prosperity Rituals of the Goddess
The Tide that Speaks
The Scrolls of Petosiris: 13 Rituals from the Feathered Eye
Petosiris and the Living Plague of Osirion
Feline Fire: Bastet's Passion and Love Magick
The Star Altar of Petosiris
Bastet's Whiskers: Supernatural Sensory Magick
The Bastet Grimoire
Feeding the Shadows
The Mouthless Prayer
The Spiral Wound
Becoming the Ibis: Lessons from Petosiris's Mind
The Crimson Coven: Cola Magick for Sweet Dominion
Sacred Cat's Paw
The Soda Zodiac: A Flavor for Every Sign
Covenant of the Crawling Flame
The Ink of Ish'Zur
Frothroot: The Thirst That Ate the World
The Golden Glyphs of Prosperity
The Etherbind Codex
Echoes of the Resistance: Reclaiming the You That Survived
Harnessed Minds: Breaking Free from Mental Control
The Eyes in the Smoke
Rootwake: The Carbon Covenant
Skitter Logic: Unlearning the Fear That Built You

Doctor Who: The World That Froths
Rootwake: The Fizz That Rewrites Flesh
Rootwake: Frothfather of the World
The Holly Pact: Blood Beneath the Mistletoe
The 2nd Mass Principle: Building Unbreakable Tribes
Web of Wits: A Survival Guide to Encounters with Anasi the Spider (Aunt Nancy)
The Hexbreaking Handbook: Effective Spells to Remove Curses
Pop Alchemy: Transform Your Life One Sip at a Time
The Mason Code: Leading in Unleadable Times
Petosiris and the Fifth Chamber of Thoth
The Ether Seed Within
The Parent of Tomorrow
Petosiris's Pyramid of Perpetual Wealth
Unlearn the World
Grimoire of the Hollow Tongue
Zodiac Weeds: Finding Your Strain Through the Stars
Aquarius Rises in the Bank
The Sugar God's Smile
The Skinclock Reversal: Biohacking the Face of Time
Debtburn: How to Obliterate What You Owe Forever
The Ice Cream Oracle: What Your Cone Says About Your Future
Silence Is Sovereignty: The Power of Being Unreadable
The Wind That Whispers Through Stone
Path of the Four Directions
Doctor Who: The Maestro's Symphony of Endings
Oxygen Grail: Breathing to Undo the Clock
Zodiacal Collapse: When Stars Devour Time
Teachings from the Red Sand Silence
Doctor Who: Omega – The Broken Equation
Memory Wipe Your Past: Start Over Like a MiB

Mitochondria Prime: Ignite the Core of Youth
A Nest of Roaches
Grub from the Galaxy: MiB Recipes You'll Never Forget
Whiskers of Power: Bastet's Guide to Inner Sovereignty
The Gift Must Cost Them: Negotiation Through Unequal Exchange
The Worm Guys' Wealth Code: Hustle Like an Alien
Bug Out: The Edgar Method for Ruthless Goal Setting
Weaving Life with Spiderwoman's Pattern
Doctor Who: The Rani's Renaissance
How to Get a Job (If You're a Puppygirl)
Speak Through Others: The Art of Proxy Power
T-Rex Your Trauma: Reclaim the Power of Your Primal Self
The Black Briefcase: How MiB Stay Wealthy in Silence
The Thirst Beyond Reason: Understanding Diabetes Insipidus From the Inside Out
Backwoods Witchcraft for Billionaires: The Pagan Path from Dirt Roads to Gold Roads
The Moonshine Grimoire: Fermented Spells for Abundance
The Nameless Geometry
The Wraith's Mixtape: Spellcasting with Songs of Sorrow
The Gallifreyan Gentleman: Silent Wealth, Sonic Confidence, and the Doctor's Code of Living
Sugar Water Confidence
Dino Totems: Spirit Guides from Earth's First Gods
Pumpkin Sigils & Ritual Smoke
The Hózhó Compass
The Distortus Discipline – Order from Inner Mutation
Witchcraft for the Cold-Blooded Soul
Moonlight Over the Blessingway
Water, Interrupted: When the Body Forgets How to Hold On
Deformed but Divine: Embracing Your Asymmetry
Hexes in the Henhouse: The Farm Witch's Guide to Power

The Reversed Flame: A Grimoire of Inverted Power

Salt, Cells, and Sanity: Reclaiming Balance with Diabetes Insipidus

King of the Broken: Crowning the Flawed Self

Moonlight Scars: Emo Moon Magick and the Art of Lunar Sorrow

Noose Spells: Magick of the Hanging Rope

The Goth Cathedral: Rituals of the Broken and Beautiful

The Cretaceous Codex: Dino Spirits and Fossil Magick

The Turkey Bones Ritual

Nine Lives of Manifestation: Unlocking Bastet's Reality Codes

Chaos Muscles: Building Strength from Twisted Pain

Emo Blood Magick: The Veins of Power

The 3AM Flood: Nighttime Urination, Sleep Loss, and the DI Spiral

The Silence Between the Stars

The Lemon Method: Sour Your Way to Success

Starlit Sovereign

The Rite of Twelve Gates: Walking the Gates of the Duat.

Cornbread and Conjure: Recipes for Riches and Rootwork

The Black Rose Rituals: Emo Love Spells and Obsession Magick

The Eternal Goodbye: Death Magick and Rebirth Rituals

Sinkrot: The Drain That Remembers

The Hybrid Mindset: Thinking Beyond Evolution

Bone Dry: Navigating Dehydration Before It Breaks You

Wreathcraft: Winter Sigils and Yuletide Spells

The Rite of Twelve Mouths

S'mores of the Damned: Haunted Recipes for Halloween Night

Rethink the Drink: A Beverage Survival Guide for DI Warriors

The Shadow Chord: Guitar Magick and Sonic

Malformed Yet Majestic: Leading When You Feel Wrong Inside
The Cursed Diary: Ink-Stained Spells of the Emo Soul
Anxiety Off Switch: Emergency Reset for a Fried Nervous System
The Energy Heist: How to Take Back Your Life from Drainers
Beyond the Bathroom: Rebuilding Your Social Life With DI
Coyote's Gift for Decision Makers
Ghoul-Goo: Spooky S'mores You'll Die For
Echoes in the Mirror: Scrying and Self-Destruction Magick
Thread and Thorn: Stitching Spells from Rural Cloth
The Mogwai Mind: Building Untouchable Wealth from Small Ideas
Be Your Own Guide: Trust Your Inner Compass
Hormones in Chaos: The Endocrine Puzzle of Diabetes Insipidus
ChronoCleanse: Detox Your Biological Timeline
The Limb You Hide Is the One That Saves You
Leaves, Bones, and Whisper Spells
The Dinosaur Mindset: Prehistoric Tactics for Modern Wealth
Clawing Back Control: A Bastet Method for Boundaries and Empowerment
Samhain Codes of the Forgotten
Orange Alchemy: The Autumnal Spellbook
Monster Within, Master Without
The Sigil That Sleeps
Hearthcraft: Yule Hearth Sigils and Winter Warmth Spells
Temple of the Purring Moon: Rituals from Bastet's Lineage
When the Earth Remembers Your Footsteps
Food for Mood: Eat to Heal Depression, Not Just Survive It
Witch of the Kudzu Vine: Southern Pagan Wealth Secrets
The Invisible Diagnosis: Advocating for Yourself With DI

The Coffin's Lullaby: Sleep Magick and Nightmares as Portals
Ashes of the Will: Rituals for Erasing the Self
The Fracture Rite: Shattering the Magickal Core
Funeral Candles: The Art of Emo Flame Magick
The Black Grimoire: A Blank Ritual for Writing in Absence
Phantom Thirst: A Halloween Survival Guide for Diabetes Insipidus
The Hollow Crown: Emo Royalty and Magick of the Outcast King
Sandpainting for the Soul
Falling Into Balance: Using the Extra Hour to Recalibrate Life
100 Southern Superstitions That Still Work
The DI Child: A Parent's Guide to Raising Hydrated, Happy Kids
The Jungle of Shame: Escaping the Hidden Lab of Doubt
The Witch's Toast: S'mores Spells and Creepy Confections
The Hoodoo Pantry: Spells from the Mason Jar
The Immortal Fortune: Secret Wealth Lessons from Captain Jack Harkness
The Specter's Embrace: Magick for Channeling Ghostly Lovers
Grateful Waters: A Thanksgiving Survival Guide for Diabetes Insipidus
The Seizure Gospel
Harvestbind: Autumn Sigils and Samhain Spells
Doctor Who: The Algorithmic Awakening
Silent Nights, Steady Waters: A Christmas Survival Guide for Diabetes Insipidus
The Extra Hour Effect: How One Hour Can Transform Everything
Blade Between the Breaths
Running with the Mountain Shadows
Echoes of the Failed Experiment – Becoming a Living Legacy

Swamp Witches & River Ghosts: Real Southern Hauntings

Cornbread Prophecies: Magical Recipes from a Southern Table

Doctor Who: The Signal in the Star

Bloomcraft: Spring Sigils and Equinox Enchantments

Vanisher: How to Disappear from the Internet Without Losing Your Life

The Ultimate Christmas Cookie Cookbook

The Unbreakable Parent: How to Mentally Survive Raising Kids in a Broken World

Time Debt: How to Reclaim the Hours You Didn't Know You Lost

One Month, One Million: Unconventional Cash Creation Tactics

Doctor Who: The Cyber Conversion Protocol

Black Friday Frenzy: The Art of Finding Hidden Online Deals

The Grimoire Buried Under the Apple Tree

Digital Couponing Masterclass: Your Step-by-Step Guide to Black Friday Savings

The Fire Inside the Flint

Shadows on the Ceiling: The Emo Guide to Astral Magick

The Bone-Eaters Beneath Us

Black Friday Bundle Blueprint: Creating Irresistible Product Packages for Maximum Sales

Thirteen Nights of Unbinding

Doctor Who: Engines of Influence

Pumpkin Spice Alchemy: Recipes of Fire and Frost

When Raptor Met Rexy: Prehistoric Lessons in Wild Romance

Oblivion's Candle: Burn the Path Behind You

Campfire Curses and Chocolate: A Halloween S'mores Grimoire

The Wallet That Wasn't Mine: Breaking Free from Inherited Scarcity

The Cola Zodiac: What Your Fizz Says About Your Fate

Frostfire Fortune: Unlocking Winter's Hidden Prosperity

Signal Jamming: Detox Your Brain from Info Overload

The Dust of the Forgotten Rite

The Golden Cat Sigils: Drawing Power in Bastet's Name

Mud Magick: The Prosperity of Getting Dirty

Savory Spicefall: Beyond the Pumpkin Pie

Pumpkin Spice Apothecary Kitchen

The Pumpkin Spice Economy: Turning Trends into Billions

The Ember Veil: 13 Nights of Fire Magick

Financial Freeze: When Earning Triggers Panic

The Gingerbread Alchemist: Sweet Recipes with a Twist

Biosynth Power: Programming Yourself from Scratch

Echoes from the Talking Circle

Truffle Alchemy: Fungus of Fortune

Spores of Power: The Truffle Witch's Handbook

Doctor Who: The Tower That Speaks

The Mycelium Veil: Truffle Magick Unbound

Broke But Ashamed: Healing the Shame Wound of Debt

The Evergreen Mind: Growth Through Winter Stillness

The Black Veil Truffle Rite

The Voice Beneath Symbols

Witchlight on the Bayou: Swamp Spells for Sovereignty

I Grew Up Poor and Now I Sabotage My Success

The Lantern of Hollow Souls

Shutdown Survival: A Citizen's Guide to Thriving When Government Stops

When Abundance Feels Like a Threat: Healing the Hidden Fears of Enough

The Scarecrow Grimoire

Owls of the October Veil

Candlewax and Curses: A Halloween Spellbook

Excavating the Inner Fossil – Transforming Fossilized Thoughtforms into Tools of Power

The Yule Witch's Spellbook: Magick for the Holiday Season

Haunted Christmas: Ghost Stories for Winter Nights

The Christmas Survival Guide: Thriving Through the Chaos

The Bone Orchard Rites

Haunted Commerce: The Ghost in the Marketplace

When Money Triggers the Inner Child

Silent Night with the Silence: A Christmas Thriller

The Lightning Crown: Living and Leading Through Seizures

TARDIS Tidings: Festive Stories from the Whoniverse

Autumn Reset: Slowing Down Without Falling Behind

The Trillion Dollar Soul: Rewriting the Currency of Reality

Truffle Eclipse Magick

Micro-Manifestations: Quick Magick That Works

5-Minute Rituals for Busy Witches

The Marshmallow Massacre: Halloween Treats with a Sinister Twist

Blood and Blackberry Thorns

Magickal Mornings: Rituals for a Blessed Christmas Day

Embers of the All-Hallows Fire

The Pumpkin Market Collapse

The Hour You Gained: Transforming Time Into Power

The Chamber Must Be Sealed: Mastering the Power of Controlled Access

The Cursed Manuscript of Petosiris

The Festive Hearth: Creating Holiday Traditions

Darkness Rising: Thriving as Nights Grow Longer

Harvesting Time: Turning the Year's End Into Your New Beginning

Petosiris and the 13th Zodiac Key

Wagewound: When Paychecks Become Identity Prisons

Walls That Watch

The Silent Feast: Rituals of Power in the Longest Night

The Distortus Legacy : Becoming a Deformed King in a Perfect World

The Hollow Masks

The Gratitude Furnace: Forging Gold from Thanks

Feast of Inner Gold: Eating for Energy and Enlightenment

Haunted Commerce: The Season of Spending Spirits

Fear Bonds: How Panic Creates Profit

Black Friday E-Commerce Playbook: Sales Tactics to Skyrocket Your Holiday Revenue

Budgeting for Black Friday: A Holiday Savings Planner

Haunting the Harvest Moon

The Warrior's Water: Emergency Preparedness for People With DI

The First Sip of the Year: A New Year's Survival Guide for Diabetes Insipidus

Doctor Who: The Thirteenth Node

The Unseen Struggle: Mental Health, Anxiety, and Chronic Thirst

The Hearth's Hidden Ledger: Counting Energies as Currency

The Gift Alchemist: Turning Any Offering Into Gold

The Papyrus of the Bound Spirit

The Magick of Leftovers: Transmutation in the Fridge

Frost and Fortune: Christmas Wealthcraft for the Modern Magus

Last-Minute Gifts: Creative Ideas on a Budget

10 Secrets to Surviving Holiday Crowds

The Witch's Dow Jones

The Witches' Graveyard Shift

Pumpkin Sigils: Carving Rites for Midnight Power

The Secret Shopper's Black Friday Guide: How to Get Early Access and VIP Deals

Fever in the Foundation
The Neuralyzer Reset: Reprogram Your Morning Routine
Lightning Lessons of the White Painted Woman
The Enchanted Snowflake
The Magic Sip: Surviving Disney Parks with Diabetes Insipidus
The One Who Draws Through You
Santa's Secrets: A Magical Holiday Planner
Silent Bells, Loud Miracles: Self-Help for the Season of Stillness
The Sugar Spell Codex: Confectionary Magick of Christmas
Autumn Hexcraft: Fallen Leaves, Fallen Barriers
Sleep Like a Fortress: Build a Life Where Insomnia Can't Survive
Nowhere Was Ever Home
Christmas Under the Stars: A Celestial Holiday Guide
Rentproof: How to Never Be Evicted Again
Workless: Escape the 9-5 Without Being Broke
The Gilded Gift: A Wealth Altar for Christmas Morning
The Black Friday Grimoire
The Hollowing: Ceremonies of Spiritual Collapse
Doctor Who: The Nameless Signal
Where the Eagle Hides His Courage
The Dwarf Tyrant's Ascent: Claiming Power in a World of Giants
The Currency of the Dead: Trading with Spectral Bankers
The Icebound Witch: Survival and Magick in the Cold
The Emergency Money Mind: Constant Crisis, Zero Calm
Thirst & Roses: A Valentine's Survival Guide for Diabetes Insipidus
Springing Into Clarity: Mastering the Energy Shift of Daylight Saving
Speed of the Nanotyrant: Agile Strategies for Life's Hunt

The 90-Day Reset: A Science-Backed Guide to Reinvent Yourself Before the New Year

The Coil of Thorns

Timegates Unleashed

Dopamine Fasting 2.0: Rewiring Your Brain in a World of Overstimulation

The Nanotyrannus Mutation: Embracing Your Differentiated Form

Unwritten January: How to Use the Blank Page of the Year to Re-Author Your Life

Feast of the Forgotten Spirits: Ancestor Magick for the Holidays

The Burnout Codex: A System for Thriving Beyond Stress

I Don't Deserve to Have Money

When the King Doesn't See You: The Shadow Predator's Guide

The Reset Ritual :A Guide to Shedding Last Year's Weight—Emotional and Physical—by Spring Cleaning Your Soul

Calendar Alchemy: Learn to Bend Time and Productivity around Your Natural Rhythms

The Mirror Contract: A One-Sentence Agreement with Yourself that Unlocks Real Change

The Nile Formula: Sacred Flow for Millionaire Minds

Forward Momentum: Productivity Rituals for the Lost Hour

Harvest Gold: Wealth Magick of Pumpkin Spice Commerce

The Magick of Christmas Lights: Illuminating Holiday Rituals

Cranberry Crown: Royal Self-Worth through Ritual Meals

Petosiris and the Worms of the Feathered Throne

The Evergreen Equation: Self-Help for Sustained Growth

The Rain Will Wash Us Away: Emo Weather Magick

Snowlight Shadows: Magick Under Frozen Stars

Doctor Who: Merger of Empires

The Light Within the Feast: Magickal Wealth of Yuletide Flame

Get Some Tarot cards: https://www.makeplayingcards.com/sell/apophis-occult-shop

Get some shirts: https://www.bonfire.com/store/apophis-shirt-emporium/

<u>Instagrams:</u>
@apophis_enterprises,
@apophisbookemporium,
@apophisscardshop
Twitter: @apophisenterpr1
Tiktok:@apophisenterprise
Youtube: @sg1fan23477
Hive: @sg1fan23477
CheeLee: @SG1fan23477

Podcast: Apophis Chat Zone: https://open.spotify.com/show/5zXbrCLEV2xzCp8ybrfHsk?si=fb4d4fdbdce44dec

Newsletter: https://apophiss-newsletter-27c897.beehiiv.com/

If you want to support me or see posts of other projects that I have come over to: **buymeacoffee.com/mpetchinskg**

I post there daily several times a day

Get your Dinowicca or Christmas themed digital products, especially Santa Raptor songs and other musics. Here: **https://sg1fan23477.gumroad.com**

Apophis Yuletide Digital has not only digital Christmas items, but it will have all things with Dinowicca as well as other Digital products.

www.ingramcontent.com/pod-product-compliance
Lightning Source LLC
LaVergne TN
LVHW022014200926
848481LV00007B/2379
9798295405372